To my friends and family—GN

To Mary and Andrew—VT

First published in North America in 2000 by

Loyola Press

3441 North Ashland Avenue
Chicago, Illinois 60657

Original edition published by Lion Publishing, plc, Oxford, England
Copyright © Lion Publishing, plc 1999

Text by Mary Joslin
Illustrations copyright © 1999 Gail Newey

ISBN 0-8294-1504-1

Acknowledgments

Luke 11:2–4; Psalm 19:2–5; Revelation 21:1, 3–4; and Psalm 130:1–4 are from the *New American Bible*, copyright © 1991, 1986, 1970 by the Confraternity of Christian Doctrine, Washington, D.C., and are used by permission of the copyright owner. All rights reserved.

Revelation 4:11; Matthew 5:43–45; and Matthew 6:24–27, 33 are from the New Jerusalem Bible © 1985 by Darton, Longman & Todd, Ltd., and Doubleday, a division of Bantam Doubleday Dell, Inc. Reprinted by permission.

Psalm 27:4; 1 Corinthians 13:4–8; Psalm 27:1, 13–14; Psalm 23:1–4; and Psalm 100:3–5 are from the New Revised Standard Version Bible: Catholic Edition copyright © 1993 and 1989 by the Division of Christian Education of the National Council of the Churches of Christ in the U.S.A. Used by permission. All rights reserved.

00 01 02 03 04 / 6 5 4 3 2 1

Our Father

The prayer Jesus taught

Mary Joslin ❖ *Illustrations by Gail Newey*

Loyola Press

Chicago

Many, many years ago, Jesus was praying. After he finished, one of his disciples said to him, "Lord, teach us to pray." Jesus said to them,

"When you pray, say:
    Father, hallowed be your name,
        your kingdom come.
        Give us each day our daily bread
        and forgive us our sins
        for we ourselves forgive everyone in debt to us,
        and do not subject us to the final test."

Luke 11:2–4

These words inspired the Lord's Prayer, or Our Father, a prayer that is still prayed by Christians all over the world.

Our Father

Sometimes,
when I am all alone,
I dream that I am not alone.

I dream that I am close
to One who loves me.

I see little children
safe in the arms of someone who loves them
and I dream of finding love like that,
strong and kind;
and I dream of finding love
that will keep me safe
forever.

One thing I asked of the LORD,
    that will I seek after:
to live in the house of the LORD
    all the days of my life,
to behold the beauty of the LORD,
    and to inquire in his temple.

Psalm 27:4

Who art in heaven

I look up at the skies
spreading wide to a great beyond—
an endless sea of stars and constellations.

Then I know for sure
there is more than I can see.

Then I wonder
what deep love
and powerful wisdom
holds the universe in place;
I wonder about the greatness
that is above the universe
and beyond it.

The heavens declare the glory of God;
   the sky proclaims its builder's craft.
One day to the next conveys that message;
   one night to the next imparts that
      knowledge.
There is no word or sound;
   no voice is heard;
Yet their report goes forth through all the
   earth,
      their message, to the ends of the world.

Psalm 19:2–5

Hallowed be thy name

Wonders are all around:
the fresh beauty of leaves,
the sparkling purity of splashing water,
the fierce majesty of the sun,
the gentle kindness of the warm breeze.

Such wonders whisper of the world's Great Maker
and call us to silence,
to reverence,
to worship.

You are worthy, our Lord and God,
to receive glory and honor and power,
for you made the whole universe;
by your will, when it did not exist,
    it was created.

Revelation 4:11

Thy kingdom come

I am looking for an escape:
an escape from all that is gray and dreary.

I have glimpsed brightness just enough—
in flashes of beauty, in words of kindness—
and I am looking
for a world made new.

Then I saw a new heaven and a new earth. The former heaven and the former earth had passed away, and the sea was no more. . . . I heard a loud voice from the throne saying, "Behold, God's dwelling is with the human race. He will dwell with them and they will be his people and God himself will always be with them [as their God]. He will wipe every tear from their eyes, and there shall be no more death or mourning, wailing or pain, [for] the old order has passed away."

Revelation 21:1, 3–4

Thy will be done on earth
as it is in heaven

I am dreaming of the world
as it should be:
where there is laughter
and kindness,
generosity and love.

Jesus said,
"You have heard how it was said, You will love your neighbor
and hate your enemy. But I say this to you, love your enemies
and pray for those who persecute you; so that you may be
children of your Father in heaven, for he causes his sun to rise
on the bad as well as the good, and sends down rain to fall
on the upright and the wicked alike."

Matthew 5:43–45

Give us this day our daily bread

All I need is
enough to sustain me
through life's great adventure,
traveling light,
traveling free,
traveling to the farthest shore.

Jesus said,
"No one can be the slave of two masters: he will either hate the first and love the second, or be attached to the first and despise the second. You cannot be the slave both of God and of money.

"That is why I am telling you not to worry about your life and what you are to eat, nor about your body and what you are to wear. Surely life is more than food, and the body more than clothing! Look at the birds in the sky. They do not sow or reap or gather into barns; yet your heavenly Father feeds them. Are you not worth much more than they are? Can any of you, however much you worry, add one single cubit to your span of life?

"Set your hearts on his kingdom first, and on God's saving justice, and all these other things will be given you as well."

Matthew 6:24–27, 33

And forgive us our trespasses

Each new day dawns
fresh and clean
and full of hope.

So many evenings end
with a sigh:
for foolishness that led to tears,
for mischief that turned to malice,
for the chances to do good
left neglected.

Then I long for these bad things
to be left behind
and forgotten.

Out of the depths I call to you, LORD;
   Lord, hear my cry!
May your ears be attentive
   to my cry for mercy.
If you, LORD, mark our sins,
   Lord, who can stand?
But with you is forgiveness
   and so you are revered.

Psalm 130:1–4

As we forgive those who trespass against us

*I do not want to be trapped
by the worst thing I ever did—
labeled and condemned.*

*I want the chance to learn,
to grow, and to change.*

*For that reason, I shall give
the same chance to others.*

Love is patient; love is kind; love is not envious
or boastful or arrogant or rude. It does not insist
on its own way; it is not irritable or resentful; it
does not rejoice in wrongdoing, but rejoices in
the truth. It bears all things, believes all things,
hopes all things, endures all things.
Love never ends.

1 Corinthians 13:4–8

And lead us not into temptation

Do not let my path
be too hard.

I do not want to find myself
in the midst of so much
wickedness and misery
that I give up believing
in goodness and love.

The LORD is my light and my salvation;
    whom shall I fear?
The LORD is the stronghold of my life;
    of whom shall I be afraid?

I believe that I shall see the goodness of the LORD
    in the land of the living.
Wait for the LORD;
    be strong, and let your heart take courage;
    wait for the LORD!

Psalm 27:1, 13–14

But deliver us from evil

Keep me safe from the things that dishearten,
the things that terrify,
the things that destroy.

The LORD is my shepherd, I shall not want.
  He makes me lie down in green pastures;
he leads me beside still waters;
  he restores my soul.
He leads me in right paths
  for his name's sake.

Even though I walk through the darkest valley,
  I fear no evil;
for you are with me;
  your rod and your staff—
  they comfort me.

Psalm 23:1–4

For the kingdom, the power, and the glory are yours, now and forever. Amen.

 In the early days of Christianity, the followers of Jesus added words of praise to the end of the Lord's Prayer, expressing their confidence in God.

Know that the LORD is God.
　　It is he that made us, and we are his;
　　we are his people, and the sheep of his pasture.

Enter his gates with thanksgiving,
　　and his courts with praise.
　　Give thanks to him, bless his name.

For the LORD is good;
　　his steadfast love endures forever,
　　and his faithfulness to all generations.

Psalm 100:3–5